God's Way
IS THE
Best Way

KATHERINE DORTCH

Hello, my name is Catalina Black. My parents are Effie and James Black,

When I was four years old my parents, and I moved to Chicago, because my father's job was relocated there. My mother did not really want to go, but, she did not have any other choice but to follow her husband.

Things were going from bad to worse, I end up having poliomyelitis, and my parents were very distraught.

When they heard the news of my illness, my mother lost her faith in God, and blamed him for my illness, my father, on the other hand became an alcoholic and a cheater.

I thought I found someone who really cared about me, but little did I know, this person was just using me, that's when I start doing things my way. It seemed like I wasn't getting anywhere, but in trouble. A friend of mines told me," Catalina, you have tried doing things your way now it's time to try and do it God way, because his way is the best way.

ACKNOWLEDGEMENT

*F*irst and foremost, I would like to thank God. Who inspired me to write this awesome book? According to Ecclesiastes 3: There is a time and season for everything, Adhere to God and trust him, because God's way is the best way.

And I would like to thank Prophet R.T Purham Senior who introduce me to God's awesome words. If it was not for him I would be like a lost sheep walking around in darkness, also at various times he would let me read my writings to the congregation at my church.

Missionary Betty Stamper, who always encourage me to keep on writing and never give up. My Pastor now R.T. Purham Jr. who keeps on inspiring me with his wonderful preaching and teaching of God words.

I would also like to acknowledge my family who I loved very much. My Mother Ophelia, My Sister, Rochelle, Helen, My Brothers,

Alexander, Napoleon, My wonderful children, Patrick, Colette, Kim, Tiffany, My Dear precious grandchildren's, the ones here in the states and the one's in

Japan, My Aunts Joelle, Rosie, Mae Gratis, Fannie, and Ruby. My sons-in-law Torrence middlebrooks, Ulysses Erving, two brothers-in-law, Anthony Miles, Jerome Jobes, Nephews, Alexander Junior, Cedric Junior, and Anthony Junior. My Nieces. Jamila, Antoinette, Angie, LaShawn, little Parrish, and all of my wonderful friends.

CHAPTER ONE

It was a very typical day at the Blacks house that morning Effie was in the kitchen cooking breakfast. James and Catalina were on the front porch, taking in that fresh, clean country air.

Effie: "James...breakfast is ready. You and Catalina come on in the house and eat.

James: "What are we having Effie?

Effie: "Well, Catalina loves her pancakes so we are having her favorite dishes: ham, bacon, rice, eggs, biscuit, grits, her delicious pancakes and also I made coffee for us."

So James, Catalina and Effie sat down to breakfast, but before they started to eat, Effie spoke.

Effie: "James, before you put that food in your mouth, put it down so I can say grace."

James: "Sorry Effie, I'm just hungry."

Effie: "It doesn't matter how hungry you are always put God first and then we eat."

So, when everyone finished eating their breakfast. Effie, asked James what was he going to do for the rest of the day.

James: "I'm going to Melvin's to ask him would he like to go fishing today."

Effie: "Well, Catalina and I are going to town so I can get her a dress for church. Speaking of church, why don't you come with us."

James: "" Effie you know how I feel about church, the things that be going on, I'd rather go fishing instead of going there. People gossiping, keeping up foolishness, members talking about each other. I'm not a Christian, but I thought church was a place where you could go to have peace and to hear God's word being preached. I didn't know it was like of those silly shows that are on television."

James, please don't take too long making up your mind about church. It's like they say you study long you study wrong I'm going to keep on praying that you will come to church soon."

So later on Effie, and Catalina went to the clothing store to get her that new dress, Effie realized that she had to pick up a few items from the grocery store as Effie, and Catalina went in the store, as Effie was about to get some milk someone taps her on the shoulder and she look around and it was Tina who she knew from grade school.

Effie: "Tina girl, where have you been?"

Tina: "I've been to Chicago, thought I might like it there, but I was wrong it was just not for me, my home is right here in Arkansas, WOW, look at Catalina she's so pretty with those big rosy cheeks, I've sure have missed you all can't wait to get back in church, you tell everyone I said hello, and I will see them next Sunday, Oh Effie I forgot how is James, is he in church now?"

Effie: "NO,

Tina: "Well, I'm going to pray that he will give his heart to God and get in church soon."

Effie: "Well, I keep trying to tell him to get in church, but James is stubborn just like a mule I'm going to keep on trying that he will get into church soon."

Tina: "Okay girl, I will talk to you later."

Immediately, after Effie and Tina were done talking, she put Catalina in to the car, and put the groceries in the back seat, then Effie drove off about hour later she was at home, Effie took Catalina out the car and grab the groceries from the backseat of the car, and then she went in the house. Effie put Catalina on the floor and sat on the couch for about ten-minutes, she Got up and put the groceries up in the cabinet. When

Effie finished putting up the groceries she started cooking dinner, when the food was ready Effie call out to Catalina in the living room She did not respond, so Effie call out to her again as she was about to go get Catalina, ther she was pulling at her dress tail.

Effie: "Catalina. Are you hungry?"

Catalina: "Mommy, where is daddy? Is he coming home?"

Effie: "Yes, he'll be back he went fishing with his friend your daddy will be back early Sunday morning so will you please eat your dinner."

So after, dinner, Effie decided that her and Catalina would go outside to enjoy some fresh air.

Effie: "Catalina, would you like to go outside for while?"

Catalina: "Yes, mother, May I bring my bike outside to."

Effie: "Yes, you may."

So Catalina brought her bike out and her mother told her not to go too far on the bike. As Effie was talking to her daughter, a car pulled up in the driveway. It was Mr. Smith her husband boss. James was a dedicated worker and his boss always told James he was one of his best workers, he work in this big plant where he made parts for cars, buses, and boats and etc.

Effie: "Hello Mr. Smith, how are you doing, what brings you out?"

Mr. Smith: "I'm fine, is your husband home?

Effie: "No he's not here; he went fishing with his friend and won't be back early Sunday morning."

Mr. Smith: "Tell, him to come to my office before he goes to work."

Effie: "Okay Mr. Smith, you have a nice day."

Mr. Smith: "You and Catalina as well."

So when Mr. Smith left Effie, and Catalina stayed outside until it was almost dark.

Effie: "Catalina, I think it's time for us to go inside, so bring your bike on in with you."

When Effie and Catalina went into the house, she took her upstairs to give Catalina a bath, put on her favorite pajamas and put Catalina to bed.

When Effie put Catalina in bed she decided to go downstairs and watch television, when a commercial came on Effie went in the kitchen to make her a cup of coffee. As she was fixing her coffee, there was a knock at the door.

Effie: "Who is it?"

Vernal: "Effie, it's me Vernal."

Vernal, was a very long time dear friend, she knew Vernell when they were young children,

Effie mom's and Vernal mother were very good friends, Vernal was like a sister Effie never had.

Effie: "Girl, what are you doing here?"

Vernal, I have something to tell you and I really need your opinion."

CHAPTER TWO

*E*ffie, you know I've been going to church for a very long time, and I've have been thinking about leaving and going to another church. Most of those people at church act just like pharaoh their hearts are hardened. The only thing I will miss is my pastor preaching, teaching sermons about God's good word, and my good friend, Effie.

The pastor will be preaching and teaching a good sermon, and half of the people will be doing other things besides listening, it just so much confusion going on in the church and it's just sad.

Effie: "Vernal, wait, I have something I would like to share with you, so please listen:"

You know you're my friend, and I just want to tell you something my mother told me before she died. Just listen and don't say a word until I finish. I came home from church one day. I said, Mom, I've been thinking a lot about leaving the church, because of all that nonsense that be going on in the house of God. I'm so tired of hearing all that mess every Sunday and Wednesday. She said to me baby listen to me, I don't care what church you go to there will always be a mess everywhere you go. Why leave as long as your heart is in it and you are adhering to the pastor preaching and teaching God's words? Don't worry about what someone else is doing or saying as long as you do your part. God sees and hears everything that goes on in his house. Vernal, if you want to leave, that's on you. I can't make you stay, you have to make up your own mind. Vernal don't be a bird brain, be a child of God."

Vernal: "Effie, what is a bird brain?"

Effie: That's when you want to fly away, and it sounds like you want to fly away. My mother would tell you this is not the time to fly away. Stay where you are and continue serving God, not man."

Effie: "Vernal, my mother loved God and her church, whenever they needed something done around the church she was always there helping out. My mother as long as I could remember never miss one day out of services, she was a God fearing woman, and so what are you going to do Vernal?"

Vernal: "With that good information you just gave, I 'm going to stay. It's like you said. I'm not going to church to hear all of that foolishness; I came to hear the word of God being preached and taught and to praise God."

Effie: "Now, that's my friend talking. Don't ever, as long as you live, stray away from God."

Vernal: "Effie, thank you. I really did need that. I'll see you and Catalina in church Sunday."

Effie: "Vernal don't do it because of me, do it for you."

Vernal: "I know, Effie. I won't be a bird brain; I will be a child of God."

After Vernal left the house, Effie went upstairs to check on Catalina. She was fast asleep. The next morning, Effie woke up early because she knew James would be home and she wanted to have a big breakfast ready as soon as he came home. As Effie was slaving over the hot stove, she heard keys rattling in the door. The door opened, and it was James with a bunch of catfish.

James: "Hey, babe, what are you doing?

Effie: "I'm making breakfast for you and Catalina this morning."

James: "Where's my little girl"?

Effie: "She's upstairs still asleep, oh yeah, your boss came out here looking for you and he told me to tell you the first thing Monday morning you come straight to his office before you start your shift he would like to talk you."

So that night Effie cooked the fish and spaghetti that James wanted, and they all sat down to eat but as Effie stated; before we eat can you please say grace.

That morning James went on in to work, but before he started his shift he went straight to Mr. Smith office.

James "Hello Mr. Smith, Effie said "you were looking for me yesterday."

Mr. Smith: "Yes, please come in and have a seat. Your wife was right, I was looking for you yesterday. James my boy, our plant is moving to Chicago, and If you want to keep your job, you'll have to move there as well. So what do you think?"

James: "I think it's wonderful, but I have to go and discuss it with my wife first, and then I'll get back with you about this."

Mr. Smith: "Well, please don't take too long. You have a week to let me know what you're going to do

James went home to discuss his situation with Effie; he really did not know how to tell her the news about the move to Chicago.

Effie: "James, what are you doing home so early?"

James: 'Well Mr. Smith, lets us leave early today. Effie, I have something that I would like to tell you.

Effie: What is it James?

James: "Well, Mr. Smith told me our plant is moving to Chicago, and if I wanted to keep my job, it would be best if I'd move to Chicago. I explained that I'd have to discuss it with you first, so that's why I'm home so early. So Effie, how do you feel about moving to Chicago."

Effie: "I'm not sure about moving to Chicago, because, I'd really miss the church, my pastor, and friends, furthermore, I don't want my daughter growing up in a big city, but James you are my husband, and wherever you go, Catalina and I will follow. So tomorrow, you can tell your boss I said yes, I will go with you to Chicago.

James went to work early so he could tell Mr. Smith the good news about leaving for Chicago. When James left, Effie went upstairs to check on Catalina; she was sound asleep. Effie then went back downstairs to make her some coffee, as she fixed her coffee she looked out her window and saw Mr. locks coming towards her house. He then knocked on the door.

It was Mr. Locks; a very dear friend of Effie's mother, whom she'd known since Effie's dad left them. When Effie was a little girl, she loved Mr. Locks as if he was her biological father.

Effie: "Who is it?

Mr. Locks: "It's Your neighbor from next door, Mr. Locks."

Effie: "Mr. Locks, how are you?"

Locks: "I'm fine, God is good, and where is my precious little angel?"

Effie: "Catalina, she's upstairs asleep."

Mr. Locks: "I heard you all were moving to Chicago."

Effie: "Who told you?"

Mr. Locks: "Well when you're in a small town, everyone sees and hears everything. So, is it true?

Effie: "Yes it is Mr. Locks, I was going to tell you, but someone beat me to it first."

Mr. Locks: "Effie, when are you all leaving?"

Effie: "Well Mr. Locks, we're leaving for Chicago in about four months, I really don't want to go, but James job is relocating to Chicago and if he wants to keep his job he will have to go since there aren't too many jobs here."

Mr. Locks: "Well I'm sure going to miss you and Catalina, you know you're like a daughter to me and Catalina is just like a granddaughter. I've known you ever since you were a little girl and now you have a little girl yourself, when you all move to Chicago make sure you keep in touch with me."

Effie: "Mr. Locks ever since my mother died you've been like a father to me, and I really appreciate everything you have done for me and Catalina. I will miss you, and we love you so much."

Mr. Locks: "I know, but remember Effie find yourself a good church home, stay there and keep faith in God no matter What. James, on the other hand, is a different story, one day he'll smell the coffee and come to his senses, just keep praying for him. Oh Effie, I almost forgot to give you this poem, read this when you feel discouraged."

Effie: "So Effie opened the note and read the poem. Oh Mr. Locks this is so beautiful, Thank you so much."

> If God brings you to it
> He will bring you through it
> Happy moments, praise God
> Difficult moments, seek God
> Quiet moments, worship God
> Painful moments, trust God
> Every moment, thank God

Four months later, they were ready to leave for Chicago, That night Effie said goodbye to all her friends in church, her pastor, especially Vernal. The next morning James, Effie, and Catalina were on the plane to Chicago, when they arrived there was his big brother holding a sign saying: James, Effie, and little Catalina.

Buck: "Hey, kids, over here"

James: "Hey bro, how have you been?"

Buck: "I'm blessed, God is good all the time."

Effie: "Yes he is, all the time."

Buck: "Hey sister-in law, this must be my little niece Catalina. She sure is a pretty little thing, she must have taken after you, because my little brother sure is ugly.

So they all got settled in Buck's home with his wife and children. All together, there were fourteen people living in that house. Time went by quickly. As James was working he managed to save his money so he and Effie could get a lovely apartment of their own. The day came when they finally moved out of his brother's home.

James; "Well big bro, It's time for us to go. I really thank you for letting us live here with you and your family until I got myself together. Bro, here's a little something for letting us stay here. Buck: Thank you and your family for putting up with us, we really appreciate it so much.

Buck: "It's my pleasure. You know, I was not going to

Let you Effie and that precious little niece live in the street. We're really going to miss you all, and don't forget to call or come over sometimes, you're not that far from me. You make take care of those girls."

James, Effie and Catalina got settled in their new home, which was very nice. Effie really loved the kitchen and the bedroom they both were big cozy looking. Catalina's room was amazing; it was fit for a little princess. About a week later, Effie called her sister-in-law, Hattie to ask her about the church she and Buck were attending.

Effie: "Hello Calvin, is your mother at home?"

Calvin: "No Aunt Effie, she went shopping with my sisters."

Effie: "Well when she returns will you please tell her to call me."

Calvin: "Yes auntie, I'll make sure I tell her to call you."

Effie got off the phone, went upstairs to checked on Catalina and got ready for bed.

Catalina: "Mommy, where is Daddy?"

Effie: "He went out for a while with his friends, he'll be back, and when he returns, I'll tell him to come and kiss his daughter, even if you are asleep. Now close your eyes and get some sleep."

Effie put Catalina to bed and went back downstairs to read her Bible.

When Effie finished reading, she went into the kitchen to make herself some coffee. As Effie was making coffee, she heard the phone ring and answered it.

Effie: "Hello."

Hattie: "Yes, this is Hattie, returning your call."

Effie: "Yeah girl, I called to see if you and Buck were going to church tomorrow?"

Effie: "Well, would you all mind picking me and Catalina up for church Sunday?"

Hattie: "Sure, we'll pick you up around eight because Sunday school starts around that time, and church service starts around ten."

When Effie got off the phone she turned around and there was James, staring at her very strange.

Effie: "James, why are you looking at me like that and where have you been?"

James: "Out with my brother and his friends."

The next morning, Effie awoke at six-thirty, went into the bathroom to wash her face and hands, and went downstairs to fix breakfast. When she finish cooking; Effie went back upstairs to get ready for church. Effie got dressed for church, and woke Catalina up, took her downstairs and fed her, when Effie finish, she bathe Catalina and put her clothes on for church. Before they left the house, she left James a note telling him his breakfast was in the oven and she would see him about two o'clock.

When everything was over at church, Buck and his family took Effie and Catalina home.

Effie: "Buck, I really appreciate you coming to get me and Catalina, thank you."

Buck: "Yeah, I was coming, but I stayed up late with Hattie watching this good movie on television. I told Hattie we'd better go on to bed so I could get up and go to church."

CHAPTER THREE

*W*hen Effie and Catalina entered the house, she called out to James, but there was no answer, so she called out to him again and still no answer. Effie then took Catalina upstairs to change her clothes. Once she finish putting her on some comfortable clothing, she took her downstairs to the living room to watch television while she went to the kitchen to fix dinner. By the kitchen being so close to the living room, Effie could easily keep an eye on Catalina."

Effie finally finished cooking dinner, and went to the living room with her daughter.

Catalina: "Mommy, where's daddy?'

Effie: "I don't know baby he'll be home after while and then we can eat dinner."

An hour had passed and James had not came home yet. Effie told Catalina to come on in the kitchen and eat dinner, as they were about to sit down, someone was rattling keys in the door; it was James.

James: "Hey, honey what's for dinner?"

Effie: "Food, James."

James: "what's wrong with you Effie?"

Effie: " You don't come in the house and talk like that, you could have said; "hello Effie and how is my sweet daughter doing"? No, you come dashing in here talking about "what did you cook."

So they all went in the kitchen and sat down to dinner. When everyone finished eating, they all retired to living room to watch television. As they were watching the TV Catalina decides to curl up on Effie.

Catalina: "Mommy, I really don't feel good."

Effie: "What's wrong baby girl"

Catalina: "My stomach, leg and head hurt. I really feel bad mommy."

Effie: " My sweet little girl, let me get some medicine for my little girl so she can feel better."

About an hour later Catalina fell asleep and her father took her upstairs and put her to bed. James went back downstairs and continued watching television with Effie , after the movie went off they retired upstairs, but before Effie went into her bedroom she went to check on Catalina; she went over to her bed she felt her forehead and it was very hot, she called out to James.

Effie: James, can you please come in Catalina room please hurry."

James: what's up babes?"

Effie: "James, Catalina is so hot, I think we better take her to the hospital."

James: "Effie, you stay here with Catalina while I go get the car and bring it around the front."

James went outside to get the car, while Effie stayed in the house with Catalina. When James pulled up in front of the house, he blew his horn so Effie could bring their daughter outside on the porch. James got out of the car went to the porch to get his daughter and put her in the backseat of the car. They then drove off to the hospital.

When they arrived at the hospital James carried his daughter right on in with Effie right behind.

James: "Excuse me please; my daughter is very sick can we please see a doctor?"

Lady at the front desk:" Will you all please have a seat and someone will be with you monetarily."

They all went back to sit down, as they were about to sit the lady at the front desk called them back to the desk, and asked "can one of you all please fill out these forms please."

About ten minutes later a nurse came out of the back and told James to bring Catalina in, when Effie finished filling out the forms and giving the lady James insurance card she went straight in the back where Catalina and James were. Fifteen minutes later a doctor walked into the room.

Doctor: "Hello, I'm Doctor Cast, my colleagues and I will be monitoring your daughter's case very closely. I see what the nurse written down on her chart, we will be taking Catalina upstairs to run some test on her, so can you please wait right here, and the nurse will be coming in shortly to get her." When they finished taking tests on Catalina, they brought her back down to her room. The nurse told Mr. and Mrs. Black Doctor Cast will be down with the test results when he finishing looking them over."

When Doctor Cast finished reading the test results, he went back downstairs to talk with Mr. and Mrs. Black.

Doctor: "I have Catalina test results and she's a very sick little girl, we will be admitting her, the nurse will be down to get her when the room is ready."

One hour later the nurse came down to take Catalina upstairs to her room with the Blacks right behind her, that night Effie and James stayed overnight with their daughter they really could not get any sleep because the doctors and the nursing were coming back and forth in and out of her room all through the night.

Doctor Earl Johnson: "Hello, I'm Doctor Earl Johnson, and these are my colleagues Doctor Denise Hubert, Doctor Verdell Dixon, Doctor Jan Dunlap, and Doctor Casey Stone. We will be in charge of your daughter's case. My colleagues and I have gone over Catalina's chart. We'll be giving her tests and also ice baths to try to control her fever, with your permission of course, we would also like to give her a spinal tap to find out what's going on."

Effie: "Doctor Johnson, what is a spinal tap?"

Doctor Johnson: "Would one of my colleagues like to explain?"

Doctor Dixon: "I will explain, It's a procedure to collect and look at the fluid surrounding the brain and the spinal cord, Suring this test, a needle is carefully inserted into the spinal column low in the back lumbar area. Samples are collected, these samples are studied for color, and blood cells counts, special proteins glucose and other substance, and they are put in culture dishes to see if there are any infections, such as bacteria or fungal growth.

Doctor Dixon: "Mr. and Mrs. Black, so we will leave you alone, and I will be back in thirty-minutes for your answer."

Effie: "James, what do you think?"

James: "Well Effie, we don't have any choice in the matter. I think we should go ahead and let Doctor Johnson give her the test."

Effie: "You are right James, we don't have a choice and we love our daughter very much and I don't like to see my baby in pain, so when he comes back we will tell him to go ahead with the test."

So Doctor Johnson came back in the room and the Blacks told him to go ahead and give Catalina the test.

Doctor Johnson: Mr. and Mrs. Black, the nurse will be down here in ten-minutes to take her up for the spinal tap."

So about four-thirty that evening the nurse brought Catalina back down to her room, and told Effie and James that the doctor will be down monetarily to speak with them, Doctor Johnson finally walked in the room.

Doctor Johnson: "Well, we gave Catalina the spinal tap and it told us what's going on with her I will explain to you all what we have found out, your daughter have poliomyelitis is an acute viral disease, usually affecting children and young adults, caused by three polioviruses, characterized by inflammation of the motor neurons of the brain steam and spinal cord, and resulting in motor paralysis, followed by muscular atrophy and often permanent deformities, since we do not have the facilities to treat her, we will have to transfer her to Chicago Children Hospital."

James: "Doctor Johnson when will this all take place?"

Doctor Johnson: "We are talking about Friday morning, but we need your consent to transfer her. I have the forms can you please make sure you read them before you sign them there's a little clause that states that Catalina will be in a room with other children and young adults who have the same disease that she has, and will not be allow any visitors other than her parents, You can only see Catalina through a window for about five minutes I'll give you all time to think about this and you have until Thursday to give me an answer. Look guys you have been here all week and have not taken a break since your daughter is asleep why don't you go home, and get some dinner in your stomach's, and a goodnight sleep and come back tomorrow."

Effie: "No, James can go but, I'll stay."

James: "I will too,'

Doctor Johnson: Well, you guys look very tired, why don't you go to the cafeteria and get something to eat."

Effie: "Okay, we will but we are not going home, if you need us for anything please have us page."

So, Effie and James went downstairs to get them something to eat. When they finished James asked Effie a question about God.

James: "Effie, can I ask you a something, can you tell me how do you feel about your God now?"

Effie: "Whatever, do you mean James?"

James: "You have been serving God all these years and look what he has done to your daughter."

Effie just sat there eating, while James went on about God, and she finally spoke.

Effie: "You know what James, you're right, all these years I have been worshiping, and praising God, doing things around the church, and he couldn't even help me."

As James and Effie were talking, her sister-in-law Hattie walked in, she heard what James was telling her about God.

Hattie" Effie, I can't believe my ears, what is wrong with you'?

Effie: "What do you mean Hattie?"

Hattie: "I spoke with your friend Vernal on the phone, and she explained to me how good of a friend you are, how you are a God-fearing woman, I'm surprised to hear what you're saying about God. I heard you and James talking, how could you be so cruel? I can understand James, but you Effie, you know better! What has God ever done to you but love you Effie. Every time something happens to someone the first thing they do is blame God. For one, they don't know him and two, they don't know what the bible says. Have you read John 10:10? Its stated: the devil comes to steal, kill and destroy, and Jesus came so we may have life and have it to the full."

As, Effie was going on James abruptly cut in on Hattie conversation.

James: "Hattie, I think you should leave and stop preaching to my wife about your precious God."

Hattie: "James, you're nothing like your brother, I can't believe my ears and Effie all the wonderful things I've heard about you, your friend vernal speaks very highly of you; how you've helped her change her mind about the church and all. How could you do this to God?

Effie: "Hattie, did you hear my husband? I think you better leave. I have enough to worry about, I don't need your input about anything, so will you please just go and leave us alone."

Hattie: "Yes, I will go and leave you alone just remember what I said, Effie and James you are going to regret everything you said about God and you too Effie because you know better."

James: "Hattie, the only thing I regret is having you for a sister-in-law."

Effie: "You know you were pretty harsh on Hattie, maybe she's right."

James: "Look Effie, our little girl is laying upstairs very sick, you don't need anyone, you have me and that's all you need all you need."

So about an hour later Effie and James went back upstairs to sign the papers so they could move Catalina to the CHICAGO CHILDREN HOSPITAL.

Nurse Gina Davis: "Hello, Mr. and Mrs. Black, I'm Nurse Gina Davis. I'll be Catalina's nurse and Doctor Chan will be her physician he sends his apologies for not being here to meet with you But he is in surgery and he told me to give you all a tour of the hospital, and will be here shortly to me with you. Oh don't worry about Catalina she'll be well taken care of so let's go upstairs and I'll show you all the room your daughter will be staying in."

So Nurse Davis took them upstairs to the room where Catalina will be staying.

Nurse Davis: "This is the room where Catalina will be staying."

Effie: "It looks like a............

Nurse Davis: "Is jailhouse the word you were trying to say, well, I can assure you its not, we may have an unusual way of treating our patients, but it works."

As Doctor Davis was about to say something else her beeper went off.

Nurse Davis: "Nurse Davis: "Excuse me; I'm being paged, I'll be right back, can you all wait here for a moment?"

Effie: "James,

This hospital seems very strange, I don't think we should leave Catalina here."

James: "Trust me, Effie everything will be alright, it's about our daughter we want her to get well , so let's not worry about this place."

When Nurse Davis came back, she took them down to Doctor Chan's office. They entered the room and Doctor Chan was sitting at his desk reading.

Nurse Davis: "Excuse me Doctor Chan, this is Mr. and Mrs. Black, the parents of Catalina."

Doctor Chan" Hello, I'm Doctor Chan, I'll be your little girl doctor, first of all we'll be taking Catalina upstairs tomorrow and treating her condition, later on we will be giving her lots of therapy, she has a lot of muscle weakness in her left leg. We will do everything in our power to help her. Nurse Davis will take you upstairs so you can say goodbye to your daughter. We'll see you tomorrow, oh Mr. and Mrs. Black, I forgot to tell you, while Catalina is in here she will be going to school as soon as we get her stabilized."

About two years later, Catalina came home from the hospital, she had to wear a brace on her left leg, and on top of that the bills started piling up. Effie did not hear from Hattie anymore and her husband started drinking and staying out every night. Effie had no one to talk to. Ever since she turned her back on God, things went from bad to worse.

CHAPTER FOUR

*W*hen I say that things went from bad to worse, that's exactly what happened, James lost his job, and Catalina had to go back to the hospital because of her breathing. They took Catalina back to CHICAGO CHILREN HOSPITAL, they explained to Doctor Chan, that Catalina was having a hard time breathing, He then explained to them that he would be putting Catalina on a breathing machine called the Iron Lung."

Effie: "What is the iron lung and what does it do?"

Doctor Chan: "Well, the iron lung is a chamber-like respirator, used in the treatment of Poliomyelitis that encloses the whole body except the head. It alternates' pulsation of highland low pressure to induce normal breathing movements of force air into and out of her lungs, Mr. and Mrs. Black, I have some pictures of the iron lung. Would you like to see some pictures of the iron lung?"

So Doctor Chan showed Effie and James some pictures of the iron lung that he will be putting Catalina on to help with her breathing.

Effie: "Doctor Chan, whatever you have to do please do it so our little girl can get better."

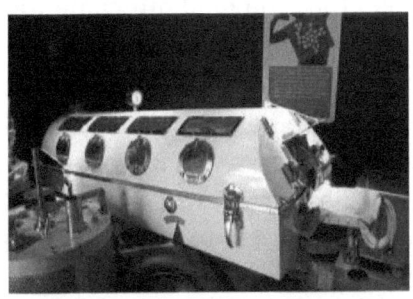

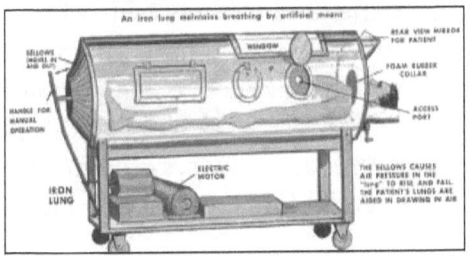

So, they admitted Catalina in the hospital again to help her with her breathing problems. Catalina stayed in the hospital for about six-months until she started back breathing on her own. That week before Catalina came home the landlord came and told Effie that they would have to move; because he wasn't running a charity house and he served them with a five day notice. You let your husband know either he come with one thousand dollars, or he can except this five day notice.

Effie really didn't know what to do because she couldn't find James anywhere. Later on that night, James came staggering in the house.

Effie: "James, you are drunk."

James: "I'm not drunk, I'm just feeling good."

Effie: "Well, feel this, the landlord came today and gave us a five day notice, and we needed to pay one-thousand dollars or move out ,your daughter will be coming home next week to what? Do you remember when we were at the hospital with our daughter when she first got sick? You told Me" all I needed was you", I don't have any friends , nothing, you took me away from me the only thing that was so important to me, and told me to trust you, but you are hardly around, do you have another family, because you sure don't take care of your family here."

James: "You know what, you worry too much, I will take care of the rent before Catalina gets home.

Effie: "I would like to know where you're going to get the money from James, you do not have any contact with your brother since you talked about his wife, I don't know why I listen to you James."

James, was doing illegal things, since he lost his job but somehow James did come up with the money, he called the landlord and told him that he had the money and to come and pick it up.

Effie: "James, where did you get that money from"?

James: "Effie, don't worry about where the money came from, you don't have to move and Catalina can come home."

So James, left the house and stayed away until Catalina came home from the hospital, little did Effie know James was having a affair with someone else, about a year later when Catalina was feeling better and everything was going fine with her, Effie decide that she should go back to school and get her education, Since, Catalina was being tutor in the hospital and around ten years old they place he in the fifth grade, even though she did not want to go to school because she knew that all the kids at school were going to be talking about her how she walked and had to wear a brace. That night James came home with two guesses' a woman and a little boy.

Effie: "James, can I speak with you for a moment, who is that woman and little boy."

James: "They, got burn out of their apartment and they have nowhere to go and they needed somewhere to stay, so I told them that they could stay here until they get on their feet."

Effie: " James, why didn't you come to me and ask me, you just don't bring people in my house without asking me."

James: "Look, Effie who pays the bills around here I do. So don't tell me who I can bring, and cannot bring into this house, and you know what, I wasn't going to say anything yet, but I 'm really tired of you, that is my son and my women so get over it and if you don't like it you can move, but Catalina stays."

So, Effie had no choice in the matter, but to live with the fact that James move in his other family, she did not have anyone, no friends, she turn her back on her sister-in-law, Effie never heard from Vernal in Arkansas because she turn her back on her too. The next day Effie went to the grocery store to get a few items for dinner, when she went down the aisles she saw Hattie, but she tried to hide from her but she saw her.

Hattie: "Effie, is that you?"

Effie: "Yes it's me?"

Hattie: " What happen to you ,your hair is really white, you have gain so much weight Effie this is not you, I cannot believe what I'm seeing, when I first saw you and James, Catalina you all were a happy couple, you had God in your life and you were a God –fearing women and you help people get there self together look what you did for your friend in Arkansas what happen to you Effie, and I heard what James is putting you through with his mistress and his son. Effie let me help you."

Effie: "Hattie, I do not need your help, will you please stay out of my business and leave God out of this, like I said I'm through with you and God, now if you will kindly move so I can check out and go home thank you."The next morning, when Effie roll over she thought James was in the bed with her but little did she know he was down the hall with his mistress and her son. So Effie got up and went into Catalina room to tell her that it was time for her to get ready for school.

Catalina: "Oh, mom I really don't feel like going, can I go tomorrow?"

Effie: "No, Catalina you will be going to school today, I know that you think the kids are going to be talking about you, but you can't stay home because of that. People talk about Jesus Christ and he kept on going and you can too, summer is over and you must get in school. Now this conversation is over ; you get in the bathroom and get ready for school I'm going downstairs to make breakfast and when you finish you come on down and eat your breakfast."

Catalina: "Mommy, is my brother going to school, today?"

Effie: "Who said you had a brother?"

Catalina: "Daddy told me that I had a brother."

Effie: "Catalina, you go upstairs and get ready for school, and I will speak to your father."

After, the kids left for school, Effie asked James could she speak to him and his friend for a moment.

James: "what is it Effie?"

Effie: "James, why don't you and your little girlfriend, be a little discrete around the kids."

When Catalina came from school she came running into the kitchen where her mother was.

Catalina: "Mommy, guess what?"

Effie: "What baby girl."

Catalina: "when, I was in school, the kids did not laugh at me or talk about my brace they said it was cool, and that they wanted one, I had a wonderful time in school today, I just can wait until tomorrow to go to school."

Four years passed, James still had his girlfriend Linda and their son in the house, Effie was still accepting James ways, he lost his job and was pretending like he was going to work every day. So that evening James came in the house staggering like he was drunk.

James: "Effie, I'm not feeling too well today."

Effie: "What's wrong James"?

James: "I don't know, I feel funny."

Effie: "Well James, if you could pull yourself from your woman for a minute, maybe you'll be able to make a doctor's appointment.

So that Monday morning James made an appointment to see Doctor Fisk. He then told Effie; he was going to take a nap and to wake him up around three o'clock.

Catalina: "Mommy, I had a good day in school today and I got a smiley face on my math paper."

James Junior: "Mrs. Effie do you know where my mother is?"

Effie: "No I don't know where you mother went, she left the house and didn't' say a word. Your dad is in the room taking a nap, is there anything I can do for you."

James Junior: "I wanted to ask my mom "for three dollars, so I could go to the restaurant and buy Catalina and I some fries."

Effie: "James Junior, look on the counter, and hand me my purse, here's five dollars, take this and go get the fries and bring my change back.

At three o clock Effie went into the room to wake James up, he got up and looked at his watch, he then asked Effie was Linda in the house.

Effie: "No, she left, and I don't know where she went, she left without saying anything to anyone. "James, what are you doing?"

James: "I'm going out to get Linda, and if she come home before I get back tell her do not go anywhere.

James went to all the clubs where he thought Linda would be, as he went to the next bar he saw his friends there so he went in.

Dave: "James, you look bad, what wrong with you?"

James: "I have an appointment to see the doctor Monday, have any of you guys seen Linda"?

Dave was one of his friends who work with him when his first came to Chicago."

Dave: "I have not seen that woman, James can I talk to you for a moment?"

James: "Sure, you can."

Dave: "James, I'm not trying to get all in your business, but I don't understand what it is you are doing. You have a nice wife, and a wonderful daughter, but yet you manage to bring another woman and her son in your home, that's just wrong James, and you know it. If you were to get sick today that woman would be gone by tomorrow and your wife would be the only one taking care of you."

James: "you know I highly respect you, but I don't need you to tell me about my life, and Linda will never leave me."

That Monday James went to see Doctor Fisk, he told the doctor what was going on with him, Dr. Fisk called for the nurse so she could take James upstairs to the lab, so they could take his blood, urine sample and also, x-ray. When James left the doctor office he went straight home. When he entered the house James called out for Linda and James junior, there was no answer from either one of them. The only person answered him was Effie she told James they were gone.

James: "Effie, Where is Linda and James junior?"

Effie: "James, all I know is Linda had her suitcase in one hand and James junior in the other, a cab was outside waiting for them, and then the next thing I know they were gone.

CHAPTER FIVE

That next Monday, James had to go back to the doctor for his test result.

Doctor Fisk: "Hello, James I have your test result back, you can come on in my office, have a seat James and I will get right down to it. Everything came back normal your blood pressure, your cholesterol is okay, but it was one test you took did not come back normal and it stated: that you have cirrhosis of the liver I would advise you to please stop drinking you have been drinking for a very long time.

As soon as James left the doctor office he went straight to the club to have a drink. Four years had passed, and James was still drinking heavily, and Effie was so confused she didn't know what to do. Catalina was about to enter high school, but it was not like the school in the hospital or grammar school; she will be entering high school where the kids will not be like the ones she knew. Finally Catalina started her first day of high school, but before the day was over the kids were very rude to her. They noticed the brace that she was wearing and they made fun of her all day, they even give her a name because of the way she walked with a limp. When school was over Catalina went straight home crying, she told her mother that she wanted to go to school where people were in the same condition as her. Effie told Catalina that she was too young to understand what she was going to say, but it was for the best. Catalina don't you ever run away from anything, God wants you to face those demons, because everything will be alright, he will always be with you just have faith and keep on moving baby. Don't worry about those kids, you deserve an education just like them, I don't care what kind of shape you are in just thank God that you are in the land of the living. James never heard from Linda or her again, but Effie ran into them at the mall, and she told Effie that she did not want to be with a sick man, and it was time for her and her son to move on with someone else. The next day when Effie woke up, she turn over to wake James up so he could take his medicine but he did not response to her.

Effie: "James, it's time for you to take your medication, still no answer, Effie got on the phone and called 911. Later on when the ambulance came the paramedics got out of the ambulance and went into the house. Effie was downstairs waiting for them, Effie told the paramedics he was upstairs in the bedroom, and was not responding back to her. The paramedics went up stairs to where James was laying in bed they tried calling out his name, but he did not answer back, they start working on him they got a heartbeat then took James quickly to the hospital. While Effie was at the hospital she called his brother and told him what had happen to James, when he heard the news he and his wife went straight to the hospital.

Buck: "Effie, I'm so glad you called me, I did not know my little brother was going through this, even though he did not want us over at the house anymore, I just feel real bad. I'm going to sit with my brother for a moment ladies, and I won't be too long. So James can get some rest. When he went in to see his little bro, he was hooked up to all of these machines. He looked down at him lying in the bed, James had tears rolling down his cheeks, he looked up at his brother Buck and tried to talk, at first he couldn't understand what he was saying, he told James to speak a little slower. James told Buck, how sorry he was that he treated his wife so bad, how he turned her away from God, and also how he talked about God. Buck I hope God can forgive me, because I was wrong, my little brother, he forgives you, and he loves you very much, now please stop talking. I'm going to leave out so you can get your rest, and I will see you tomorrow, Buck before you leave can you do me one more favor? Can you please pray with me? I need to do this, I don't know how to, can you help me please, so Buck prayed this prayer with James, and this is how it went, Jesus, I now realize I have sinned against you. Please forgive me of my sin. Please come into my life and change my heart. In Jesus name I pray Amen.

I feel so much better Buck, it seems like a weight has been lifted off of me?"

Hattie: "Effie where is Catalina."

Effie: "She's at school I told her to go on to school if anything changes I will come up to the school and get her." two months later James died, when everything was over Effie had to get a job so she could take care of herself and Catalina. So that night Catalina was in the kitchen in a corner her mother came into the kitchen and saw her sitting in the corner,

Effie: "Catalina , what's wrong?"

Catalina: "I miss dad so much."

Effie: "Effie, I miss him to but, everything is going to be alright."

So the next day Effie went to work, Catalina was at the house doing her homework for school, and all of a sudden someone knock on the door. Catalina looked out of the window and it was her aunt Hattie.

Catalina: "Aunt Hattie, what are you doing here, you know mom is still angry with you."

Hattie: "I came to see you; I knew your mother was at work. Are you alright Catalina, do you need anything?"

Catalina: "NO, auntie may I ask you something, why are you and mom not talking to each other

Effie: " Catalina, I 'm not angry with your mother, but I feel that you should talk to your mother about this situation not me well I'm going to go before you mother comes home and again if you need anything just give me a call."

Later on that night Effie, came home from work she look so tired.

Catalina: Mother, wants wrong?"

Effie: "I'm just tired, baby they really worked me hard today. Catalina would you do me a favor?"

Effie: "What is it mom?"

Effie: " Catalina, can you please do me a favor, I'm so tired and baby I don't feel too well so can you please go to the store for me, we need a few items for dinner."

Catalina: "Mom, I really don't want to go."

Effie: "Please Catalina, I really need you to do this for me."

Catalina: "Mommy, I have something that I would like to ask you before I go too the store."

Effie: "What is it baby?"

Catalina: "Mommy, why are you mad, at Aunt Hattie."

Effie: "Did Hattie say anything to you?"

Catalina: "No mom, she just came over today to ask me did I need anything and to let her know."

Effie: "And what else, Catalina?"

Catalina: "That's it mom, are you going to tell me why you are upset with Aunt Hattie"?

Effie: "Not, today, one day I will tell you alright, now will you please go to the store for me?"

Catalina: "Okay mom, I'll go but, I will go out the back way, because those girls from school are out there and I don't want them to see me, all they do it talk about me wearing a brace and how I walk."

Effie: "Okay, Catalina, but you be careful and thank you."

So, Catalina we on to the store to get a few items that her mother wanted, she went on through the alley so no one would notice her, Catalina thought that she looked very hideous; wearing that brace on her right leg, and when Catalina walked she limp, when she made it to the store she went down the aisle to get the items that her mother needed, as she was about to check out Catalina forgot one item, she went back down the aisles to find the product that her mother needed, when Catalina found the item she went to the checkout counter, so as soon as she got out of the door Catalina ran right into one of the girls at the school.

Girl: "Hello, Catalina

Catalina: "How do you know my name, are you one of the girls at school, who be with the other girls that be laughing, and talking about me?"

Girl: "Yes, my name is Tracy and I do be with those girls. I tell them that is very cruel how they talk about you, it's not your fault you have to wear a brace and walk with a limp, I also I told them that's not funny at all."

Catalina: "Well, do you hang with those girls."

Tracy: "One of those girls is my cousin Brenda, and the others girls Rose and Delores, I have been around them every since I was in kindergarten."

Catalina: "Oh, I see, well let me get this one last item for my mother, so I can check out and go home."

So, when Catalina finished she went back down the alley and someone was calling her.

Tracy: "Wait, my mother is giving me a birthday party, would you like to come."

Catalina: "I don't know your cousin, and those other mean girls will be there."

Tracy: "Please Catalina, don't worried about my cousin Brenda and the other girls, I promise you I will take care of them, you just come on to my party.

So what do you say? Are you coming to my party, it will be next Saturday; there will be boys at the party and my favorite two friends will be there; Trent and Calvin. Will you please come you can even tell your little friend Yvette to come."

Little, did Catalina, know that those means girls were setting her up. They had been planning to get her for the longest they even paid Trent and Calvin to pretend like they really care about Catalina and Yvette. I really don't know why the girls were angry with Catalina and Yvette they were some cute little things and smart, and I think that they were jealous even though Catalina wore a brace and walked with a limp. So, when Catalina made it home she went running in the room with her mother with full of excitement.

Catalina: "Mommy, guess what?"

Effie: "Catalina, I'm not in any mood to guess, what it is.

Catalina: "Mommy, I have been invited to a birthday party and another girl at my school."

Effie: "Who invited you all to a birthday party?"

Catalina: "You know those girls, who go to my school; well one of them invited me and Yvette to her birthday party."

Effie: " Catalina, I'm really surprise at you, why do you want to go to a party the way those girl's be talking about you and your friend if you want to ask me they are up to no good Catalina and they are going to hurt you, I advice you not to go to that party. Beside I have to work that day."

Catalina: "Mom, you do not even know when the party is."

Effie: "I don't care when it is, you are not going, so let's not talk about anymore?'

So, Catalina got on the phone and called Yvette and told her that her mother say that she could not go.

Catalina: "Yvette, I have a plan anyway, I'm going to that party, I just will not tell my mother that I am going so are you going did you ask your mother could you go."

Yvette: "Yes, I did and she said yes."

That whole week Catalina didn't say too much to her mother, since she wouldn't let her go to the party. As Effie was getting ready for work that Saturday Catalina was upstairs pretending she was asleep, but little did Effie know she was planning to sneak out of the house and go that party. When Catalina heard Effie slam the door, she ran to the window in her room, she saw her mother going down the streets to catch the bus. When she saw her mother leave the house Catalina ran downstairs to the phone and called Yvette to let her know that she will be at her house shortly. When she made it to Yvette's house, she asked Yvette could she call Tracie to let her know they were on their way very soon. When Tracie got off the phone with Catalina she ran quickly into the living room and told everyone that Catalina and Yvette would be their way very soon. Tracie ran to the bedroom and called Trent to let him know that Catalina and Yvette will be over soon, and to call Calvin and let him know as well. There were so many people at her party including her cousins Brenda, and Rose. Tracie told the girls to be nice to Catalina and Yvette until she give them the signal to be mean to them.

Tracy: "Catalina, girl I though you weren't coming, since you are here are you hungry."

Catalina: "Yes"

Tracy: "Oh, Catalina and Yvette I'm so glad that you all came you girls just have some fun and I will talk to you later. There is food over there on the table, you all go over there and fix you something we have chicken wings, potato chips , punch, fruit salad and more so go over there and help yourself girls."

So Catalina and Yvette went over to the table and fixed them something to eat, after they finish fixing their plates they went over in the corner to eat their food, as they were eating Trent, and Calvin came over to talk to them.

Trent: "Hello, ladies my name is Trent and this is my friend Calvin, may we sit down here with you all."

Catalina: "sure you all can sit where you please we do not own any seats here."

So, Trent and Calvin sat down with Catalina and Yvette, Trent all of a sudden he started up a conversation.

Trent: "This is a very nice party."

Catalina: "Yes, is sure is."

Trent: "Trent who is your friend?"

Catalina: "This is Yvette; we go to the same school."

So, as time went on everyone was enjoy themselves. So later on that night Trent as Catalina would she like to dance?"

Trent: "Catalina: would you like to dance."

Catalina: "No, thank you."

So, Calvin ask Yvette and she said yes.'

About ten o'clock everyone left the party. Calvin walked Yvette home, but catalina told Trent not to walk her home she could walk her on self home."

When Catalina made it home, her mother was not there so she went straight upstairs and went to bed. That morning Catalina went downstairs to make breakfast and by her surprise there was her mother in the kitchen making breakfast.

Catalina: "Mom, what are you doing?'

Effie: "What do it look like I 'm doing. I'm making breakfast so sit down and eat.'

Catalina: "Mom, can I ask you a question?'

Effie: what, is it baby?

Catalina: "Mom, remember when I asked you why do you hate Aunt Hattie, and you told me you would tell me about the situation later, well can you tell me now?"

Effie: "I don't hate her, I miss Hattie so much but I know that I was wrong a while back when you were sick and I was acting like a fool, she was only telling me right and I had to listen to your father which he did not know anything about God. But I did and I turn my back on God and I am so ashamed."

Catalina: "Why don't you call Aunt Hattie and apologize to her."

Effie: "Catalina, I will call her and apologize, but before I do anything, I have to ask God for his forgiveness."

Catalina: "Mom, I'm so proud of you."

So, Trent never gave up on Catalina he had to prove to the girls that he was committed to do what they ask of him, Calvin on the other hand really did like Yvette. When Effie went to work the next day Catalina was at home sitting in her corner as usual."

As Catalina was sitting in her corner someone was ringing the doorbell, Catalina went to went to answer the door.

Catalina: "who is it?"

Trent: "It's Trent, Catalina will you please open the door."

CHAPTER SIX

*T*rent: "It's me, may I come in for a minute. I have something that I would like to talk to you about. Catalina I do like you a lot, you are so pretty.

Trent kisses Catalina, and she kisses him back, little did Catalina know, the girls were outside waiting for Trent to let them in the house. So in the heat of passion, Catalina told Trent she was going upstairs to make herself comfortable and to give her ten-minutes and then come upstairs, little did Catalina know, Trent and the rest of the crew were going to set her up. Trent let the girls in the house and told them he would take care of Catalina so they could come upstairs and hide in the closet, leave the door open a little while they videotaped her and Trent. When they finished Trent told her to come with him in the bathroom so they could wash up together, while they were doing that the girls came out of the closet and went downstairs out the front door.

The next day Tracy called Catalina, and told her she was having a barbecue at her house and would she and Yvette like to come, Catalina and Yvette were having so much fun. Even Trent was there, but there was no Calvin. He was tired of the games they were playing.

Tracy: "let's all go in the house and watch a movie

So everyone went in the house to watch a movie, but little did Catalina know it was about her with Trent. As they were watching the movie it stop and another movie came on it was Catalina and Trent, oh Catalina was so embarrass she just couldn't stop crying so she ran out of the house and went to her house, when she got there her mother was in the living room sitting on the couch.

Effie: "What's wrong Catalina?

She explained to her mother, what was going on, Catalina also told her mother that she went to the party and she told her not to.

Catalina: "Mommy, I 'm so sorry I have really mess up."

She told her mother that she went to a party tonight, and that she had slept with Trent and how they had humiliated her they even showed this movie with me and Trent in the bed together.

Effie: "Catalina you brought this own yourself, know you are going to have to pay the price for this.

Six weeks passed, Catalina had not come on her menstruation, so she decided she would go the doctor and find out what was wrong. Catalina took blood test and a urine test. The next following week she went back to the doctor to get her test results. Catalina found out that she was pregnant, she said to herself how am I going to take care of a baby when I have not finish high school, I can't afford to take care of a baby. Over the next several days Catalina wanted so much to tell her mother that she was pregnant, but she just could not bring herself to tell her mom what was going on with her. Catalina finally discussed her situation with her mother; her mother asked Catalina did she tell Trent about the baby, she told her mother that she did not talk to Trent about the baby only her. She told Catalina she should tell Trent about the baby, because he is a part of the baby too. Catalina told Trent about the baby, and he told her he didn't want to be a part of the baby life or hers, because he loved Tracy and after high school they were going to get married. When Catalina finished talking with Trent she ran into her friend Yvette.

Yvette: "Catalina, why are you looking so sad? Your mother told me you went to see Trent to tell him about the baby, I guess he gave you some bad news, well Catalina shake it off and let it go girl and let God that boy don't know what he want, you know what that boy don't know what he want, you just trust God he's all you need and besides, your mother will help you Catalina, all you have to do is go ahead and finish school and get yourself a good job, I bet your mom's will watch the baby while you do this, and maybe you can take some college classes."

Catalina decided to go to church with Yvette and she really enjoyed herself, listening to the pastor preaching God's good words. When service was over her friend Yvette asked Catalina how was the services and did she enjoy herself, Catalina told her she liked the service and that she was going home to tell her mother, and try to get her back in church. So months passed and Catalina never heard from Trent again. Catalina began going to church with her mother. Effie made a big step and asked Hattie to forgive her because she was a fool to ever listen to James. That next month Catalina had her baby, which was a little girl, as Catalina was lying in her hospital bed she was wide awake. Catalina heard a voice telling her to write down these words, but Catalina ignored the words and turned over on her other side, again the voice came again this time it was louder. Catalina jumped up looked into the desk by her bed and took out a sheet of paper, a pen and started writing down the words the voice told her to. When she finished this is what it stated:

MY GOD, MY GOD
MY GOD, MY GOD
You are so great,
MY GOD , MY GOD
When things go wrong,
You give me strength to carry on!
MY GOD, MY GOD
Don't let me stray,.
MY CHILD, MY CHILD
I'll be with you always!

Catalina, was so astonished, she call her friend Yvette, Catalina could not believe what was going on.

Catalina: "Hello Yvette, this is Catalina, I have something that I'd like to tell you, it's very important so will you please just listen while I tell you, and I'm not crazy just listen Yvette. As I was lying here in my hospital bed, I heard voices so I got up and looked around the room, I didn't see anyone, so I looked out of the door into the hallway and there was no one there, I got back in the bed and turned over to the other side of the bed and the voice came back again, this time it was louder than before. Yvette, I jumped up in bed, turned over and looked into the desk by my bed and got out a piece of paper and a pen, and I started writing down the words the voice was telling me to. It was a beautiful poem you must come out here and read this poem tomorrow."

Yvette: "Good afternoon Catalina, okay let me see that poem you were talking about last night. This is an awesome poem Catalina do you understand what God is trying to tell you in this poem."

Catalina: "Yes, God is trying to tell me "please don't stray and he will be with me always."

When Catalina got out of the hospital with the baby, she called Yvette and asked her to stop by the house after church could she bring her some scriptures to read until she was able to come back to church. About six weeks later Catalina, her mother and the baby went to church, there was Hattie, and Buck sitting in the front seat .When church services was over Yvette said to Catalina, you know girl ever since I've know you. You have been trying to do things your way, now don't you feel good knowing that you can do things God's way and not your way "because God's way is the best way!

FINAL WORDS

Everything Has Its Time
To everything there is a season,
A time for every purpose
Under heaven:

A time to be born,
And a time to die,
A time to plant,
And a time to pluck what is planted;
A time to kill,
And a time to heal;
A time to break down,
And a time to build up;
A time to weep,
And a time to laugh;
A time to mourn,
And a time to dance,
A time to cast away stones,
A time to gather stones,
A time to embrace,
A time to refrain from embracing;
A time to gain,
A time to lose;
A time to keep,
And a time to throw away;

A time to tear,
And a time to throw away,
A time to tear,
A time to sew;
A time to keep silence,
And a time to speak,
A time to love,
And a time to hate;
A time of war,
And a time of peace.